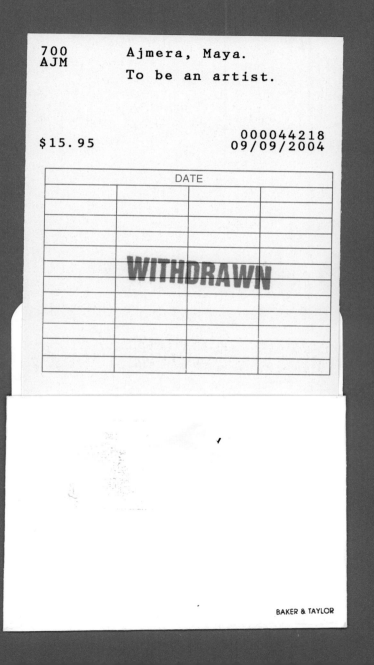

700
AJM

Ajmera, Maya.

To be an artist.

$15.95

000044218
09/09/2004

DATE			

BAKER & TAYLOR

To Be an Artist

Maya Ajmera & John D. Ivanko

Foreword by Jacques d'Amboise

SHAKTI for Children
 Charlesbridge

Mexico

The Artist and a Sense of Wonder

Have you ever thought of what a wonderful word "wonder" is? It describes the heart and mind filled with amazement: Oh, I'm so happy; I feel wonderful. It expresses curiosity about the world: I wonder what makes fire hot? I wonder what's out there on the other side of the stars? It expresses our inner thoughts: I wonder what she is thinking? I wonder if he likes me?

Wonder is generated from the grand in size—the stars, galaxies, and universe—to the tiny—the molecules, atoms, and particles. Wonder comes from the experiences of your life, your consciousness, and the relationships you make with other people. All individuals are evolving and wondering, creating the story chapters of their lives moment by moment—just as you are, even as you read this book. Wow! What a wonderful miracle is the human being!

How do we humans best express these feelings and the sense of wonder that comes out of us? We make art. We invented it: music, dance, drawing, painting, sculpting, architecture, drama, storytelling, poetry, song, and literature. These arts touch and change our lives, opening up our hearts and minds to all kinds of possibilities. Every time you use art to communicate, you become an artist, expressing the wonders of being human.

—JACQUES D'AMBOISE

FORMER PRINCIPAL DANCER OF THE NEW YORK CITY BALLET

FOUNDER OF THE NATIONAL DANCE INSTITUTE

To be an artist means expressing yourself in many different ways.

France

Tanzania

Art can be just about anything. Painting, singing, dancing, playing music, and writing poetry are popular forms of art around the worl But so are acting in a play, telling a story, weaving a basket, or making a sculpture out o clay. Dressing up, making sandcastles, taking photograph . . . these are all ways you can show your creativity.

China

Colombia

United States

To be an artist means drawing and designing . . .

Iraq

Japan

France

Vietnam

There are lots of ways to make a picture. You can use paint, pencils, crayons, chalk, or markers. You can start from scratch or color in an outline. The thoughts and feelings you have and the way you combine your subject, colors, and textures are what make your pictures works of art.

. . . and coloring and painting.

India

United States

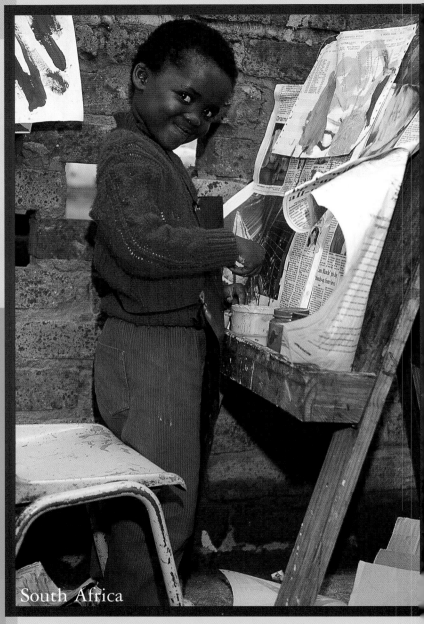

South Africa

Ukraine

Playing with colors is a lot of fun. With a swirl of a brush, you can mix blue and red paint to make purple, or mix yellow and red to make orange.

You can paint almost anything anywhere— on a canvas, a wall, or even an egg.

Ecuador

To be an artist means making music— playing drums of all shapes and sizes . . .

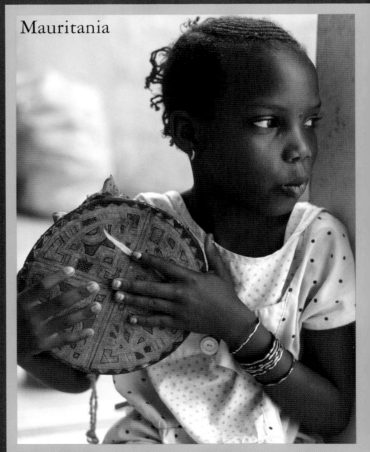

Mauritania

Indonesia

India

Jamaica

United States

Music is fun to listen to, dance to, sing, and play. It can be happy or sad, slow or fast. Anyone can be a musician. You can play all kinds of musical instruments.

United States

. . .or blowing on horns and flutes. . .

Finland

Indonesia

Peru

They can be big, like a tuba, or small, like a kazoo. You can even use your own body as an instrument to sing, hum, tap, and whistle.

Germany

Bhutan

. . . playing with little strings or big strings . . .

China

India

Slovak Republic

United States

Spain

Whether they like to sing, play, or listen, people all over the world like to get into the rhythm of music.

. . . or singing songs.

Japan

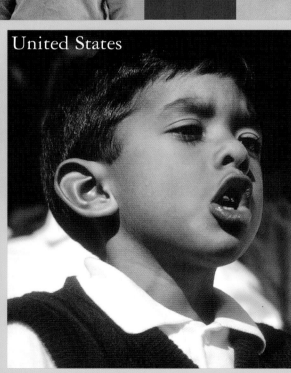

United States

Singing is popular around the world. You may sing songs at school or in a rock band. Others may sing a hymn in a church choir. But sometimes, it is just fun to sing in the shower or while taking a walk.

Sweden

United States

To be an artist means dancing your favorite steps and moves . . .

All over the world, people dance at celebrations, on stage, or while listening to the radio. You can dance by yourself, with friends, with a partner, or in a group. Moving your body to music allows you to have fun and let your feelings out. Some dances have special steps.

United States

Cuba

Eritrea

Cambodia

Spain

Austria

Japan

. . . or performing traditional dances at festivals.

Canada

Mexico

Federated States of Micronesia

Many cultures have traditional dances to celebrate special occasions. You may wear colorful dresses or costumes and have certain steps that reflect the meaning of the dance. Other dances you can make up as you go along.

To be an artist means writing a poem or story . . .

Pakistan

Bolivia

Nigeria

You can express many things with words. Poems, stories, and plays are all forms of art. Your poem or story can be published in a magazine or made into a book. Your play can be performed by actors on stage.

United States

Philippines

India

. . . or acting in a play.

You are an actor or thespian when you perform in a play or movie. Before the opening show, you have to rehearse your lines for many days. You may also wear a special costume to become a certain character.

To be an artist means sculpting a work of art,

United States

weaving a basket or colorful cloth . . .

Tanzania

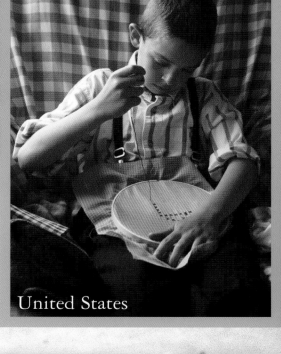

United States

Using clay, you can sculpt a bowl or an animal. With sand, you can create a castle. You can chisel a piece of rock to make jewelry. Kids weave to make colorful cloth or baskets out of leaves. Sewing different patterns on to a cloth is called embroidery. With all these forms of art, you use your fingers and hands in intricate ways.

Bhutan

. . . or stitching a unique pattern.

Mexico

To be an artist means sharing your artistic flair . . .

United States

South Africa

India

Bulgaria

United States

Thailand

. . . for others to appreciate.

Poetry readings, dance and musical recitals,
puppet shows, or plays allow others to experience
your creative spirit. Paintings, sculptures, or
photographs can be exhibited in a gallery for
others to enjoy at any time. You can perform
on stage in a theater, an auditorium, or your home
no matter where you live.

To be an artist means celebrating who you are and how you see the world around you.

Anyone can be an artist!

India

United States

Croatia

China

Art is an important part of every culture. We create art to set a mood, share our feelings, or explain what we think of the world around us. We use art to express our hopes and dreams, our desires and our points of view. Almost anything can become art that reflects our creativity and talent.

United States

India

Indonesia

CANADA

UNITED STATES

MEXICO

CUBA

JAMAICA

COLOMBIA

ECUADOR

PERU

BOLIVIA

artist in . . .

SLOVAK REPUBLIC

SWEDEN
FINLAND
GERMANY
UKRAINE
FRANCE
SPAIN
AUSTRIA
CROATIA
BULGARIA
IRAQ
CHINA
JAPAN
PAKISTAN
BHUTAN
INDIA
ERITREA
THAILAND
VIETNAM
CAMBODIA
PHILIPPINES
FEDERATED STATES
OF MICRONESIA
NIGERIA
INDONESIA
TANZANIA
SOUTH AFRICA

Iraq

Germany

Nigeria

Bhutan

United States

Sweden

To Be an Artist is dedicated to Life Pieces to Masterpieces of Washington, D.C. —M. A.

For the "seventh generation of children on earth."—J. D. I.

To Be an Artist is a project of SHAKTI for Children, which is dedicated to teaching children to value diversity and to grow into productive, caring citizens of the world. SHAKTI for Children is a program of the Global Fund for Children, a nonprofit organization committed to advancing the human rights and dignity of young people around the world. Visit www.lifepieces.org to learn more about Life Pieces to Masterpieces, a grantee partner of the Global Fund for Children (www.globalfundforchildren.org).

Developed by SHAKTI for Children/Global Fund for Children
1101 Fourteenth Street NW, Suite 910
Washington, D.C. 20005
(202) 331-9003
www.shakti.org

Published by Charlesbridge
85 Main Street
Watertown, MA 02472
(617) 926-0329
www.charlesbridge.com

Details about the donation of royalties can be obtained by writing to Charlesbridge Publishing and the Global Fund for Children.

Library of Congress Cataloging-in-Publication Data
Ajmera, Maya.
  To be an artist / Maya Ajmera, John D. Ivanko ; editor, Yolanda LeRoy.
    p. cm.
Summary: An introduction to using various art forms to express creativity.
  ISBN 1-57091-503-2 (reinforced for library use)
  1. Arts—Juvenile literature. [1. Arts. 2. Creative ability.] I. Ivanko, John D. (John Duane), 1966– II. LeRoy, Yolanda. III. Title.
NX633.A36 2004 700—dc21 2003008154

Printed in Korea
(hc) 10 9 8 7 6 5 4 3 2 1

Display type and text type set in Garamond No. 3
Color separated, printed, and bound by Sung In Printing, South Korea
Production supervision by Brian G. Walker and Linda Jackson
Designed by Susan Mallory Sherman

As always, my deepest thanks to John Ivanko for his constant support and creativity. Thank you to Joan Shifrin and Kelly Swanson Turner of the Global Fund for Children for their support as well.
—Maya Ajmera

I wish to thank my ever-cheering wife, Lisa Kivirst, and my son, Liam Ivanko Kivirst, who let me take a break from playing together to complete this book. It has been such a wonderful creative partnership to work with Maya Ajmera and to share in her vision of what the world can become, one child at a time.
—John Ivanko

Our thanks to all the photographers who participated in this project. Without the photographs, there would be no book. Many thanks also to Jacques d'Amboise and Elle Hauck of the National Dance Institute. Financial support for this project has been provided by the Flora Family Foundation, W. K. Kellogg Foundation, and generous individual donors.

PHOTO CREDITS
Front cover: © Lindsay Hebberd/Woodfin Camp. Back cover: left, © Dinodia/Ravi Shekhar; top right, © John Russell/Network Aspen; bottom right, © Kim Newton/Woodfin Camp. Title page: © David Hiser/Network Aspen. Page 2: courtesy of the National Dance Institute. Page 4: left, © John Russell/Network Aspen; right, © Network Aspen. Page 5: top, © Barbara Bussell/Network Aspen; middle, © Victor Englebert; bottom, © Lawrence Migdale/Photo Researchers. Page 6: large, © Nik Wheeler; inset, © Cameramann/The Image Works. Page 7: left, © Stephanie Maze/Woodfin Camp; right, © Mary Altier. Page 8: top left, © DPA/MAA/The Image Works; bottom left, © Andrew M. Levine/Photo Researchers; right, © Elaine Little. Page 9: left, © Mike Douglas/The Image Works; right, © Elaine Little. Page 10: left, © Kal Muller/Woodfin Camp; right, © Lauren Goodsmith/The Image Works. Page 11: left, © Yva Momatiuk/John Eastcott/Photo Researchers; top right, © Dinodia/Ravi Shekhar; bottom right, © Paula Lerner/Woodfin Camp. Page 12: top left, © BKA/Network Aspen; bottom left, © Nik Wheeler; right, © Mary Altier. Page 13: top left, © Tony Savino/The Image Works; bottom left, © Hideo Haga/HAGA/The Image Works; right, © Jon Warren. Page 14: large, © S. D. Manchekar/Dinodia; inset, © Bill Bachmann/The Image Works. Page 15: left, © John Eastcott/Yva Momatiuk/Woodfin Camp; top right, © B. Seitz/Photo Researchers; bottom right, © Robert Frerck/Woodfin Camp. Page 16: left, © Nik Wheeler/Woodfin Camp; right, © Bob Daemmrich/The Image Works. Page 17: large, © Masakatsu Yamazaki/HAGA/The Image Works; inset, © Syracuse Newspapers/Dick Blume/The Image Works. Page 18: left, © Sisse Brimberg/Woodfin Camp; right, © Betty Press/Woodfin Camp. Page 19: top, © Lorraine Chittock/Aramco World; bottom, © Mike Yamashita/Woodfin Camp. Page 20: top left, © Kim Newton/Woodfin Camp; bottom left, © Oliver Bolch/HAGA/The Image Works; large, © Nicholas Devore III/Network Aspen. Page 21: left, © Eastcott/Momatiuk/The Image Works; top right, © David Hiser/Network Aspen; bottom right, © Nik Wheeler. Page 22: large, © Jon Warren; top, © Jon Warren; bottom, © Betty Press/Woodfin Camp. Page 23: left, © Bachmann/Photo Researchers; top right, © Elaine Little; bottom right, © Salaam Baalak Trust. Page 24: large, © Monkmeyer/Press; top, © Ken Heyman/Woodfin Camp; bottom, © Syracuse Newspapers/The Image Works. Page 25: left, © Jon Warren; right, © David Hiser/Network Aspen. Page 26: top left, © Louise Gubb/The Image Works; bottom left, © Mukesh Parpian/Dinodia; top right, © John Russell/Network Aspen; bottom right, © Steve Benbow/Woodfin Camp. Page 27: left, © A. Ramey/Woodfin Camp; right, © Richard Nowitz. Page 28: left, © Nik Wheeler; top right, © Dinodia/Ravi Shekhar; bottom right, © Jeffrey Aaronson/Network Aspen. Page 29: top left, © Jeffrey Aaronson/Network Aspen; bottom left, © David M. Grossman/Photo Researchers; right, © Lindsay Hebberd/Woodfin Camp. Page 30: first row left, Ken Heyman/Woodfin Camp; first row right, © Mary Altier; second row, © David Hiser/Network Aspen; third row, © John Russell/Network Aspen; fourth row left, © Bill Bachmann/The Image Works; fourth row middle, © Eastcott/Momatiuk/The Image Works; fourth row right, © Kal Muller/Woodfin Camp. Page 31: first row left, © Nik Wheeler; first row right, © Hideo Haga/HAGA/The Image Works; second row left, © Betty Press/Woodfin Camp; second row right, © Jon Warren; third row, © Bachmann/Photo Researchers; fourth row, © Masakatsu Yamazaki/HAGA/The Image Works.